LEADING THROUGH LIVING

I0086157

11 LIFE LESSONS TO ACHIEVING
SUCCESS FOR COACHES, BUSINESS
LEADERS, OR ANYONE STRUGGLING
WITH UNLOCKING POTENTIAL

ROGER & HUNTER GOFF

LEADING THROUGH LIVING © November 2015

By Roger & Hunter Goff

Editor: Caitlin McClellan

ISBN-13: 978-0692562666

ISBN-10: 0692562664

For more information about the book or the author

Please visit huntergoff@leadinthroughlivin.com

First Edition for print: November 2015

ABOUT THE AUTHOR

After several years of leading one the most prominent youth baseball development programs in the southeast, the team splits apart to pursue college education. Fast forward just two years: when the sudden death of a friend, player, and teammate tragically hits close to home, these two (Father-Son) feel a heavy burden to leave a legacy for their lost friend. This book is a stamp for his legacy to live on forever in the hearts of his friends, family, and whoever reads this across the world. #DoItFor3 *We love you Trev, we miss you, and we think about you every day of our lives.*

Roger Goff

Moving all over the place and never having a stable home, growing up was never easy for Roger. He was forced to mature and fend for himself at a young age. He was never fed with a silver spoon, like a lot of kids are in this day and time. Hard work was the only thing he knew.

At the age of 25, Roger married the love of his life. Soon after, he and his wife, Cindy, welcomed a newborn baby boy (Hunter) to the world. Just a few years later, he had moved himself up to a highly touted management position within the company he worked for. While there, he received several "Manager of the Year" awards. His leadership was second to none in the company and he was rewarded for it.

As his son grew up to fall in love with the game of baseball, so did Roger; like any good father would. After years of watching from outside the fence, he decided to become a coach. What he didn't know was that he was about to create something bigger than himself. When Hunter was at the age of 8, he started his own youth baseball player development program. It wasn't pretty at times, as it took time to build a foundation to build off of.

10 years later, Roger had built one the most highly touted programs in the state. With his great leadership skills, he built a program of high integrity and character.

Hunter Goff

Growing up in a small town along the coast of South Carolina, Hunter had his dreams set on making an impact on the world. He knew he had a message within him that he wanted to share with people. He had often been called an 'outlier' amongst his peers, at the mention for his desire of a greater purpose in life.

At the age of 18, Hunter enrolled at The University of South Carolina where he studied Business Administration and Art Studio. At the age of 21, he started a painting business with Young Entrepreneurs Across America where he ran a $50,000 business in 6 months. He had the most marketing exposure of over 256 managers nationwide with 3 newspaper articles, 2 Live News Shows, and a meeting with the South Carolina Secretary of State pertaining to his successes. Very proudly, he was amongst the 25 of 52 managers within the Southeast Region to finish the program.

Hunter is currently on the heels of graduating college, when the next step of his journey through life starts. He has made a firm statement about being an 'outlier' by writing his first book by the age of 22. He has dreams of speaking to people across the world on being successful in life. One thing is for sure, if he stays on the track he is... Those dreams are going to come true very quickly for the young man.

DEDICATION

This book was written in the memory of a great friend, player, and teammate Trevor Worden.

CONTENTS

CHAPTER 1

INTRODUCTION

I want to start off by saying that you've made a great decision by opening up this book. It's been on my heart for a few years now to write this. I'll be honest with you though, it's something I didn't think I would be able to handle. I knew I had to though, it was just a matter of time.

Just to give you a quick background of who I am, my name is Roger and I am a proud father and husband with two kids. I have a 22 year old son and a 32 year old step daughter. My son and I, Hunter, wrote this book together with the goal of speaking to coaches and business leaders on the subject of leading people through life lessons.

Is This Book for You? Yes, Absolutely

Throughout this book, I will focus on certain life lessons that I have applied directly into our coaching and leadership styles, which have helped us become more successful and promising leaders. I'm going to get to the roots of leading a team from the very bottom with less talent than the majority of teams you will or have already played. We will get you to the top!

And you're going to hear from Hunter as he shares some inspiring words and stories from his experiences over the past couple years. You're going to see things like humility, discipline, intimidation, confidence, and failure, among a few others as you progress throughout the book.

But before we get into the good stuff, I want to give you a little insider and background information on myself so we can connect and you can understand what our story is all about.

By the time Hunter was at the age of 8, all he wanted to do was play baseball. My wife had mentioned to me a few times that I should start a baseball team. I didn't really think too much of it, but as time passed, the idea kind of grew on me. As a few months went by, I made up my mind to give it a shot and see what happened. And so I did just that.

We named the team the "Myrtle Beach Angels." Hunter fought me about naming the team the Braves, after the professional baseball team Atlanta Braves, but something told me I needed to call it the Angels so that's exactly what I did. Later on, I'll tell you why the "Angels" became kind of a cliché, a perfect fit for our team.

Because I had been managing 7 or 8 people at work for several years, I felt like I knew a good bit about coaching. But I also had a feeling that coaching kids and a game that I didn't exactly know the science of, would be a little bit different. However, I was ready for the challenge.

When Hunter was at the age of 8, I went out and found some young kids who played with him in recreational ball and that is pretty much where we started. Finding kids to play was a challenge because nobody knew who we were. The majority of the time we barely had enough kids to play, 9 or 10 kids usually. Every once in a while we would get an extra kid who wanted to join in and play with us. We usually played weekend tournaments, and would typically play 2 games on Saturday and 2 on Sunday. The tournaments would start on Saturday mornings and end sometime early in the afternoon on Sundays. During the first few years winning seemed nearly impossible. Don't get me wrong though, we won every once in a while and even had a few runner-up trophies to hang our hats on. But let me tell you, in those few years, we certainly lost more games than we won. It sucked. I hated losing. I hated losing more than I loved winning, and let me tell you, there's a difference. The few games we had won were against teams of our level or lesser. We just didn't have the talent to be able to compete with the better teams in our age division. But as we kept playing games, weekend after weekend, year after year, things slowly began to click for us. We still didn't have the most talented team around, but we started to figure out how to play together. And then all of a sudden, it seemed, we began to win games.

A few wins turned into more wins, which turned into a lot of wins. And those few runner-up trophies that we proudly received in the first few years multiplied. Heck, we had even started winning a few tournaments here and there. When we won our first tournament, it hit me. I had done it. I had finally done it! The seed I had planted when I first started this team years ago had finally grown out of the dirt into something of life. We started receiving phone calls from players who wished to play for us. By about 11 or 12, our program was established and other local teams knew who we were. Even after only these few years of coaching, I began to understand what it was all about. It was about relationships.

I cared for them, and they knew I was there to help them and support them in order to achieve success. Most importantly, I trusted them and they trusted me.

One of the main things that I found to be important was finding a way to incorporate life lessons into coaching those boys and leading my employees at work. Because no matter what sport you are playing, it is just a game. And no matter what job you work, it is just a job.

Fast-forward a few more years to when the boys were about sixteen. By now, we had one heck of a team. We had even upset the #1 team in the country out of Mooresville, North Carolina. The team we had then was pretty talented. We had some of the most talented kids in the area and even a few from out of town.

From the Bottom to the Top

We had kids like Tanner English, who played centerfield at The University of South Carolina. He now plays for the Major League Baseball team Minnesota Twins organization.

Richard Carmichael, who is now a U.S. Marine. Trey Keller, who now works for Lowes Home Improvement in App Development.

Nick Franza, who is pursuing his Pharmaceutical Degree from The University of South Carolina.

Ryder Tipton, who is pursuing his Jurisdiction Doctorate at The University of South Carolina School of Law. Let me tell a pretty cool story about Ryder. He was the only Angel, besides Hunter, who played with us from the first game we ever played until the last game. 10 years with us! Isn't that crazy?! Needless to say, we got to know each other very very well!

Even my son Hunter, who is also still a student at The University of South Carolina. While a full time student, he had his internship with "Young Entrepreneurs across America" where he actually operated his own business and oversaw $50,000 of sales throughout.

Now, these are only a few kids that came through my program. And the reason I even began to write this book was because of a young boy that played for me for many years. His name is Trevor Worden and he was, by far, one of the most special kids that I ever did know. I was thankful that I had the opportunity to coach such an incredible young man. This book was written in its entirety in memory of him.

This kid made such an impact on my life that I saved an entire chapter for him and the difference he made in my life. But I don't want to spoil it too early on by telling you his story. So, let's just put that on hold for a little bit. I'll come back to it, I promise.

Major Impact

See, everything that I'm about to tell you has had such an impact on my life that I know for a fact it will have an impact on yours as well. Maybe even you will take a thing or two out of this and apply it to your everyday life. Coaching these young kids changed my life for the better. It helped me understand just what coaching and leading people was all about.

LEADING THROUGH LIVING

It doesn't matter if you are a little league baseball coach or a Major League baseball coach, or even an owner of a small business or large corporation, you will learn from my experience. The strategies that I have developed throughout my years of coaching are what I'm about to share with you. You are going to receive the best tips and guidelines for creating success. You might even learn a thing or two from the life stories Hunter and I will share. Although we wrote this book for coaches to read and be enlightened with, anyone can take something away from this. The life lessons that I am going to focus on apply for any aged player, student, employee, or business owner. So, basically what I just told you is that you've made a great decision by opening up this book. I wrote this just for you, where ever you are in the world right now.

So let's get to it. What do you say? Each chapter in this book focuses on a specific life lesson that I have incorporated into my coaching style over the years. I am going to give you everything I know and have experienced through my past and present, to help you receive a better understanding of what coaching from the heart is all about. I hope this inspires you and touches your heart as much as it does mine. I'm going to be as down to earth and honest as possible, so here we go! Enjoy!

CHAPTER 2

What's Wrong with the World

I'm going to get right to the point with this. I'm not going to sugar coat it and make it sound like something it is not.

I see so many things going wrong in this world. So many people do other people wrong. Sometimes it is even people they "care" about. I'm sure you see things like this every day just like I do. Just turn on your TV. You can turn it to just about any channel.

For example, ESPN. Every now and then, if you are watching a Major League baseball game, you might see benches clearing from both dugouts, or maybe just a couple players getting in a heated argument over something. Heck, sometimes they're even on the same team. But, when you watch these types of things you're probably just like me and everyone else in the world watching. We sit in laughter and think to ourselves, "I wish I was there, that would be awesome to see!", "that kind of thing sells tickets, people like excitement!" or something of that nature.

And I'll be honest about it. Yes, it is pretty exciting to watch crazy things like that happen. And yes, it most likely does sell more tickets. But here's the icebreaker, not a lot of people actually take the time to realize why these types of things are happening.

See, the problem is actually pretty simple. The single-handedly most important thing to be taught is being humble. And even more important than being humble is staying humble. Being humble begins with respect. Starting with respecting yourself, it then becomes about respecting your teammates, respecting your coach, and then about respecting your competitor.

Controlling the Situation

I used to tell my players to treat others the way you would like to be treated. I can't tell you how many times I gave them this piece of advice. That's just the way I was raised growing up as a young boy and it never left me. I know it sounds simple, but it's the truth. Because it seems like such a simple thing, a lot of coaches tend to ignore it or just simply forget about it. I've seen it time and time again. Players throwing bats, helmets, gloves, you name it.

All because they struck out, popped out, or grounded out. And it all starts with one player. That's all it takes.

If the coach doesn't control it right then and there, then you've got trouble. And when that one player does it, the whole team sees it. When the coach doesn't say anything to that player, it begins to appear like an acceptable thing to do for the rest of the team. So, what happens now?

Another player does it after he grounds out to the shortstop. Just like the other, he sees it as an easy way to release his frustration. And then, all of a sudden, another player decides he wants to pull a similar stunt. Now, as a coach, you have three or four players with attitudes you have to get control of.

Do you kind of see how this sort of thing starts to become like cancer to a team?

Don't let me mislead you though. I had my fair share of problems while I was coaching. I had players who didn't want to listen just like any other coach. It's normal for attitudes to flare, at any age. Heck, I even have an attitude sometimes. It's normal, yes, but it's not acceptable. No matter who you are. When someone has an attitude about something, it stems from them not respecting themselves. It's a mindset. A mindset where they think that acting disrespectful is okay. But it's not okay for three reasons.

1. It makes themselves look bad.
2. It makes their teammates look bad.
3. It makes their coach look bad.

Most of the time, situations like these are to be handled one-on-one away from the team or anyone else involved with the team. But sometimes it's good for the other team to see you disciplining them. You might even have to bench players like this for a game or two to get your point across. Once your team sees you lighting into one of the players for having an attitude, they usually get the point that you aren't going to put up with it.

Once a player overcomes this obstacle it becomes nearly a thousand times easier to coach them. They begin to understand what respect is and how important it is. But as a coach, or leader, you can't stop there. You have to be diligent. You have to tell them over and over and over about these kind of things. If you tell them enough times, they will eventually become receptive to what you are saying.

Staying In Their Ear

Just stay in their ear about being humble. Being humble is the key to the door of success. Just be humble. Humble. Humble. Humble. This might seem a little over the top, but it's not.

LEADING THROUGH LIVING

Once you have preached it so many times that they're tired of hearing it, that's when you know you're doing something right. You should be coaching these types of things to your team before and after games. You will want these things to be a part of your pre-game and post-game team meetings while you have the entire team focused at your attention.

Once you have gotten it through the heads of each player giving you trouble, it is going to give your team a boost. And it is going to make your life easier as a coach.

Teaching humility is important because it helps in building team chemistry. The players begin to get along a little bit better after each and every practice and game. They begin to help each other out when they see their teammate struggling, which makes coaching a lot easier for you because players begin to step up with leadership skills.

When these things start happening, the competitor seems invisible. What I mean when I say "Invisible" is that the players on your team are so focused on themselves and their teammates that they are not worried about the other team. They will not care what they look like, how big or small they are, what they are doing, or what they are saying, during the game.

When the competitor becomes invisible to your team, it's a sign of respect. It's a sign of respect to the competitor, as well as to you as the coach, and the game itself. But most importantly, this invisibility is a sign that you are teaching humbleness the correct way and you are on the right tract to becoming a successful coach.

CHAPTER 3

Don't Underestimate Discipline

Not Putting Up With the Crap

This starts when a child is born. It is the parents' job to tell their child not to do something. Maybe a simple slap on the wrist that suggests they better not do a certain action again or five minutes in timeout. And when they do something good, they should be rewarded for it. This concept is applied throughout all ages of life. It is called discipline. What I'm about to tell you is very important, so focus in as much as you can right now. During my years of experience, I found that discipline became one of the most important aspects of coaching baseball.

Coaching discipline is a lot easier than most people think or try to make it out to be. There is one element to discipline. Yes, only one. And here it is:

Know your each of your players' roles.

Knowing your players' roles in situations is easier than you think. You just have to know what the situation is and what abilities your players have.

See, each player on your team will develop his or her own identity. So what that means for you is that each one of them will fall into their own place. But not overnight. It takes time, and lots of it. You know the saying: "Rome wasn't built over night" right? Well, the same applies here.

This process is very important in teaching discipline. Everything I've told you so far is very important, because it all ties into the end result, success. Or winning. Once you have figured out what players can play where and how to use your team as a whole to achieve maximum success, that is where you begin to see the light at the end of the tunnel. It is kind of where 2 and 2 adds up to be 4.

So, when you feel like you have reached this point, take it as a stepping-stone to success. Reward yourself! Go out to dinner or to Krispy Kreme. Something!

What I'm about to tell you now is probably going to blow your mind. Or at least throw you for a loop.

Why? Because it is so simple.

LEADING THROUGH LIVING

Don't Make It Harder Than It Is

Once you understand what kind of team you have and what each player brings to the table for you, that's when you can really push for discipline. And it's actually very easy the way I teach it. There are two methods of discipline that work best for me. I taught the same ones for years and they never failed me. I guarantee you that if they have worked for me for all of these years, then they will certainly work for you. The two methods I'm about to proclaim to you are crucial for your entire team to live and breathe by. Here they are:

Do what's best for the team, first.

And then do what's best for yourself, last.

Doing what's best for the team just means coaching your team to be selfless. Coaching them to play as one. Not to play "with" each other, but to play "within" each other.

Doing what's best for yourself is the same exact concept, except on the opposite end of the spectrum. (This is the last part of this chapter, but it is also the most important.)

A team will never reach its potential until each player has practiced and prepared with maximum effort. Practice does make perfect, I don't care whom you are or where you are from. And it is up to each and every player to make this happen, but it's also up to you as a coach to guide him or her in the right direction.

Through coaching these two simple methods of discipline, you and your team will know and understand how to win against the competitor. Each player will understand their roles and abilities, as will you. And you will also understand how to use their roles in certain situations to win games consistently.

CHAPTER 4

DON'T BE INTIMIDATED

It Ain't the One with the Fastest Car, It's The One Who Refuses To Lose

I learned this from the famous NASCAR Legend Dale Earnhardt. I'm sure you either watched him race at some point, maybe saw him on TV, or recognized him by the number "3" on his car. Many people knew him as "The Intimidator." I watched him race numerous times and let me tell you something about Dale. He was the kind of competitor who spectators either down right loved, or just straight up hated his guts. He simply did whatever it took to win. And he wasn't afraid of anybody, no matter who he was or how fast their car was. "It ain't the one with the fastest car who wins, it's the one who refuses to lose."

Dale Earnhardt had it figured out. He had the desire to win more than any of his competitors. He had the will to win. I started using him time after time to my players to push the intimidation factor out of their minds. Throughout my years of coaching, my players stuck to 4 basic rules. We would go over these rules in every single pre-game meeting we ever had. I repeated these rules an obnoxious amount of times because they needed to hear it. Here they are:

1. Believe in yourself
2. Trust in your ability
3. Desire a challenge
4. Your competitor is your motivation

I have lived and would die by these 4 rules. They were my bread 'n butter for getting the boys pumped up and ready to play. I remember sometimes telling them, "I believe in you. You wouldn't be on this team if I didn't. All I need you to do is believe in yourself and your ability to play." The way I saw it was, if I could get them to focus on themselves and their ability, they would be less focused on the other team. Simply put, I just thought it gave us a better chance to win.

Chomping at the Bit to Take on the Goliath

I wanted them to chomp at the bit to play the bigger and better teams. See, over the years we became the team nobody wanted to play because I had preached this over and over and over. I had instilled this competitive factor into their heads and it gave them a completely new and improved mindset.

A mindset that said "We can do anything if we just put our mind to it." It wasn't always easy for us though, because we hardly ever had the most talent. Sometimes we had to fight and claw to find wins. And that's okay. My players and I both learned a lot from it. We won a lot of games as the underdog because we simply played smarter and worked harder than the other teams we were up against.

It doesn't matter what profession you are in, who you coach, where you coach, or even what you coach. These concepts work; they have proven themselves. It is not always about teaching statistics or looking at a stat sheet all the time to figure out what player is performing at what level.

Although, that is what it comes down to at times. It is about teaching them through storytelling and teaching them the right ways to live, so that they can be successful not only in baseball, but in their life. It's all about the bigger picture here.

CHAPTER 5

GLOWING WITH CONFIDENCE

Some People Can Just Glow at Ease

Have you ever met someone in your life that just has a glow about him or her? The kind of person who has a smile on their face day in and day out? The kind of person who doesn't let anything or anyone bring them down? It's the type of person who has such an inward peace about them, that they can fight off negative things when they happen. The kind of person who isn't spoiled by success, who finds that "even-keel" attitude from remaining humble. Remember the chapter you read on being humble earlier? Well, this is where it begins to come into play.

The kind of person that I have explained to you is someone with confidence. I know this because I have met a few people like this in my life. I'm sure you have too.

There's just a sparkle about them, and you can tell that they will be successful wherever they go or whatever career they may choose.

But hang on. Let me stop for a second and explain something. I'm not saying that I know everything. Or that I'm some kind of psychologist. I think you kind of understand where I'm coming from though. Everyone has confidence. Some just have more than others. Some people love being inside their so called "comfort zone", which is where they feel the most at ease. And others love being outside their comfort zone, which is where they (in contrary) feel the most at ease. Confidence is a direct result of not being affected by intimidation (which is what we talked about in the previous chapter) and having humility (which is what we talked about in the 2nd chapter).

What Confidence Can Do For You

For me, having confidence boils down to two different things. Three distinct advantages:

> 1. Feeling better about yourself
> 2. More likely to become a leader

Getting your players to buy into the concepts of intimidation and humility is extremely important; because by doing so, their confidence will begin to increase within themselves as well as each other. This is also going to help a lot with team chemistry and getting the team to play together as one.

There's no secret code to teaching confidence other than what I just told you. If you do your job by applying intimidation and humility into your coaching scheme, this part will follow naturally. It is all interconnected.

If you are as competitive as me, then you know the immediate feeling after a big win. Think back to backyard football or video games with your friends, as a kid. I'm sure you can recall some of those times playing each other, just wasting away the day, maybe the summer months as a kid when you didn't exactly have to work yet. I remember those days. Winning was probably the best feeling in the world. It just made me feel better about myself. There was nothing else like it for me. And I don't know about you, but it has followed me throughout my entire life.

Feeling better about yourself gives you more confidence. And the more confidence someone gets, the more likely they are to step out of their comfort zone to reach for something more.

As a coach, it is our job to match our coaching scheme of confidence with our players' everyday lives.

I wanted my players to take that confidence onto the baseball field as well as into their homes and schools. I wanted my players to be able to use that confidence to their advantage in the future; in school, college, and meeting the real world by facing real jobs and bills.

Direct Advantages

A direct advantage to teaching this confidence is that your team will receive a long lasting effect and it will help them become more successful in life.

As for my son Hunter, he would have never thought that by age 22 he would have already ran a $50,000 business as a full time college student and write a book.

He says, "If you would have told me four years ago as I graduated high school, that by this age I would have already ran a $50,000 business and written a book, I would have probably laughed right in your face. I would have called you an idiot and walked away."

He has told me that my coaching methods have given him more confidence than he ever wished of having. Running that business was one of the most humbling experiences he has ever had.

Between the group of employees he had working for him, the customers he was able to take care of, and the obstacles he overcame, Hunter feels like he learned a lot from the experience and that there is no doubt it will help him in his future endeavors.

I feel confident that I have played a role in not just my son's success, but my other players' success as well, by teaching them these valuable life lessons. Just taking the time to teach these kids things like humility, discipline, intimidation, and confidence comes back and gives you the biggest gift in the world. I know I told you before that one of the best feelings is winning, but I lied. Knowing that I impacted these boys' lives and have contributed to them becoming more successful like my son, is the best feeling in the world. It is a gift that keeps on giving, that you can receive, if you just take the time to incorporate valuable life lessons like these into your coaching.

CHAPTER 6

HARD WORK BEATS TALENT, WHEN TALENT DOESN'T WORK HARD

Did you read the title of this Chapter?

Everything you need to know is found in the title of this chapter. "Hard work beats talent, when talent doesn't work hard."

I love talking about this. I could talk about how hard work pays off for days. Without end.

I'm not going to give you any bullet points to follow for this one because I believe there are none. It's as simple as this; you either want success, or you don't.

Just because someone is more talented doesn't mean that they are necessarily better than you. It just means you have to work harder to achieve the same level of success.

"Hard work beats talent, when talent doesn't work hard."

I can remember preaching this over and over and over in just about every single practice. If there was one phrase that I used more than any other, it would have to be this one. The kids responded to this the best, because they believed it. They trusted me so much as a coach, and they would do anything I asked of them. They trusted the things I told them because they knew I wouldn't lead them in the wrong direction.

Looking back on the lessons I taught them, they probably appreciated this one the most. Comparing where they were to where they are now hits a special place in my heart because I truly poured out my heart to these kids. And to see them excel to where they are now is about the coolest thing in the world to me.

Leading Through Living Our Lives

Now, just so you are aware... Hunter and I both are about to dive head first into a couple of stories that we hold close to our hearts... Here we go! One of the most special moments I experienced while coaching the Angels was a tournament we played back in the year of 2006. I can remember this day like it was yesterday. It was an early Saturday morning on October 21st. We were scheduled to play the #1 team in the country out of Mooresville, North Carolina, the Mooresville Racers. At the time, we were ranked #17th in the nation. It was an 8 am ball game and it was to be played at the Myrtle Beach Pelicans Baseball Field, which was an affiliate of the Atlanta Braves at the time.

Given that the majority of the kids were Braves fans, they were pretty excited as you can imagine. And I can't lie; I was pretty excited too! As young as they were at the time, playing on this field in this type of scenario was somewhat of a pipe dream to them.

Hunter was the starting pitcher, so as you can imagine as a dad and coach, my nerves were up the wall to begin the game.

Our offense got off to a great start in the first few innings, and we managed to score a couple of runs, which helped Hunter settle in and get into a rhythm.

We held a close lead for the majority of the game, leading 3-2. Mooresville had bigger and faster players, but we held them at par for the most part. A couple of close calls here and there along with a few great defensive plays helped us out and kept the momentum on our side.

Mooresville made a push though, towards the end of the game.

Going into the last inning the score was tied with us being the home team, which meant getting the last chance to bat. This also meant if we held the Racers scoreless and we somehow managed to score a run, we would automatically win.

Before they all took the field at start of the final inning, I brought the team together in a huddle. I told them that this was their time to shine, the time all their hard work is going to pay off, and to go out there, have some fun, and make it happen.

It must have been our lucky day because we held Mooresville scoreless to start the inning. When Hunter threw his last pitch to record the last out, I knew there was some magic in the air. Because my last click on my pitch-count clicker (which just keeps track of the amount of pitches that are thrown by your pitcher) was 100. I thought it was too good to be true! Like what are the chances of landing on that?!

We come up to bat and ended up winning in dramatic fashion. With one out in the inning and runners on 1st and 2nd, one of our players Hugh comes up. After our runners steal 2nd and 3rd, Mooresville decides to intentionally walk Hugh (that means is automatically putting the batter on 1st base by throwing four intentional balls to a standing up catcher standing far enough from the plate that the batter shouldn't be able to reach the pitch). The count was 1-0 (1 ball, no strikes), so all they had to do was throw three more and put him on base to have a force play at each base, giving them a better chance of keeping us from scoring.

The first two pitches were thrown well off the plate to the standing catcher.

Let me explain something real quick about the way an intentional walk is supposed to be handled by a batter. The batter is supposed to stand and watch the pitches come in, with no intention WHATSOEVER of swinging the bat, much less hitting the ball.

Okay now that I have laid that out for you, let me tell you how this goes down.

The second ball comes in. Ball 2.

The third ball comes in. Ball 3.

Now the count is 3-1.

As a coach in this situation standing down the third base line, I'm thinking about how I'm going to approach the bases being loaded with one out to make sure we get a run across the board to win this thing.

As ball four is being thrown, I'm just assuming Hugh is going to stand there, let it go by, and take his base.

Well, it was anything but that.

The pitch came in a little closer than the first two and Hugh decided to swing the bat. I hear the "ping" of the bat hitting the ball and then see the ball going into the air.

And it's almost as if someone had taken this moment and put it in slow motion. It stayed in the air just long enough to fall in the outfield over the heads of the second baseman and shortstop, just like a miracle. We had won the ballgame 5-4 and the boys went wild running on the field in celebration of victory.

This was definitely my favorite moment as a coach, because all of the hard work had paid off for us. The way the game started and the way it ended was somewhat of a romantic. There are certain moments in life where you just know when they happen that it's going to be something you'll always remember. This was definitely one of those.

Hunter has a pretty touching story for you to hear too. He wasn't sure whether or not he felt comfortable telling this story because he holds it so close to his heart.

So here he is:

I about had to beg Dad to let me get a word in here. I hope you've enjoyed hearing all of this inspiration so far with all of the stories and different things that I'm sure you've been able to relate to, in some way or fashion.

I could sit here and tell you story after story of how I've learned all about what hard work is from the lessons Dad taught me growing up. But there's one story of mine that sticks out to me more than any other and I want you to hear it.

Last summer, in 2014, I had an internship with a company called "Young Entrepreneurs across America", where I operated my own business and oversaw $50,000 worth of revenue come in. The business model was an exterior house painting business through their household name 'Student Painters'.

In October of 2013, the company hired me on, but not before a strenuous three- interview process.

Once I was hired, I spent the next few months leading into January formulating a business plan with how I was going to recruit, market, manage, etc. It ended up being a lengthy twelve page business plan.

At the end of January, I went to a two day training seminar that the company held for us. Here they taught us everything from sales, recruiting, hiring, leadership, etc. It was the whole nine yards. They gave us everything we needed to know to go out and start our business.

While I was there, I got to meet all of the interns from the North and South Carolina regions. There were about 45 other aspiring college students just like me. As I began to meet them one-by-one I started to realize just how special of a program I was a part of because they all had that glowing confidence about them.

After that two day seminar was over, we were off to starting our businesses.

Here's how it worked for me. I would travel back and forth every single weekend from college, where I was taking full time classes, back to Myrtle Beach, which is where I had decided I wanted to build and run my business. Myself included, there were about twelve other interns at USC, and two executives who split us up into two teams and managed us.

It was quite the challenge taking full time classes and running my own business all at the same time, as you can probably imagine.

During the first few months, we had company standard sales goals we had to meet, or else we would get released from the program. The first couple of goals were $20,000 and $25,000 during the first few weeks of May. I passed these with flying colors as I was sitting pretty at $33,000, or so I thought.

At the beginning of June, there was a $30,000 goal that had to be met. Three days before that deadline approached, I lost two jobs, which sunk me back down to $26,000. I thought there was no way on Earth I was going to meet this deadline. I was ready to throw in the towel and quit.

LEADING THROUGH LIVING

The deadline happened to land on a Monday, which gave me that weekend to make something happen. I only had Friday, Saturday, and Sunday.

I scheduled nine estimates for the weekend, and with my average sale coming in at $2500, that meant I had to go at least two for nine to push me back over $30,000. Five estimates were scheduled for Saturday and the last four for Sunday. Saturday morning rolled around and I jumped out of the bed fired up and determined to make this thing happen.

I scattered my estimates throughout the entire day so that I could concentrate on each customer and wouldn't feel rushed. As determined as I was about overcoming the letdown, it didn't seem to work. I went 0-5 on Saturday with no sales and only four estimates left on Sunday to reach the mark.

As I drove home from that last estimate on Saturday, I was angry. I was angry about a lot of things. I didn't know what I was doing wrong or why this was happening to me, because I had already put in so much effort towards my business that I didn't want to quit. But with the deadline two days out and after hearing five no's in a row, I couldn't see the light at the end of the tunnel. All I saw was darkness.

As I laid down Saturday night, I prayed and hoped that tomorrow would bring me some better luck.

And as I climbed out of the bed the next morning, I looked at myself in the mirror and said "Today, I can't accept no. I just can't."

But it didn't happen. At least not after my first estimate. It was a dreadful no, even after I brought up several objections. I felt hopeless. There were many emotions stirring in me that I felt like a volcano ready to erupt. As I hopped back into my truck to leave that customer's home, I completely lost it. As I began to turn the ignition to crank the truck, my head just collapsed onto the steering wheel.

Tears came bursting out of my eyes, dripping onto the steering wheel and then onto my pant legs. As I sat there for a minute or two I began to calm down. I decided to call Dad because I needed someone to pick me up and who better, I thought, than your own Dad-Coach combo.

He gave me some words of advice that sometimes the going gets tough, but you have to keep on keeping on. And that now was one of those times. What happened next was unbelievable. The next three estimates were all sales and it trumped me back up to $34,000. I literally felt like I was in a dream, it was that surreal to me!

The point of me telling you this story is that hard work pays off. It truly will pay off in the long run if you just have patience and keep working towards your goal.

LEADING THROUGH LIVING

I had heard six no's in a row, can you imagine that?? I could've threw in the towel and quit. I could've quit after the first no. Or the second no. Man, what about after that third no. Did I want to? Absolutely I did. But I didn't. I kept on moving forward, even though I felt like I was spinning my tires in the mud.

So my message to you, is to keep going. No matter what it takes, just keep going. If you're team is in a slump or they just can't find a way to win, keep pushing them. It might not make sense today, tomorrow, or the next week. But it'll make sense in three months, four months, a year, or two years from now. You just have to keep on keepin' on when the going gets tough. Because at the end of the day, the saying reigns...

"Hard work beats talent, when talent doesn't work hard."

As this chapter concludes, I'm going to give you back to Dad and let him take back over. Here he is:

I hope you've relished his inspiring story as he's told it to me several times. This kind of leads right into the next chapter where the focus gets thrown on failure and our need to embrace it.

CHAPTER 7

FAILING FIRST

Don't Be a Runner and Hider, Be a Riser

Failure is a funny thing, because everyone is scared of it. Everyone runs and hides from it, like they expect to find succeed without failing first. And that's why the majority of this world just settles for less than what they are actually capable of. Heck, this might even be you right now. We all have doubts about certain things and that's okay. But the thing that isn't okay is misinterpreting the affect that failure has on us.

See, the problem is we don't understand failure and how it actually helps us. Throughout the years, I found two different reasons why failure is important and how we can use it to help us. Here they are:

1. It's when we learn the most about ourselves.
2. Understanding the difference between embracing and desiring failure.

Whether we want to believe it or not, failure helps us. One moment of failure gets us one moment closer to success. When we fail at something, you either quit or you keep going. It brings about a decision in which we learn the most about ourselves. We either lay down or we get up and keep fighting.

This was one of the biggest takeaways Hunter experienced during the last story he told you. He learned that he wasn't a quitter. He had the will power within him to keep on pushing through that dark tunnel with a firm trust that he would see the light eventually.

After taking in both of these stories in the last chapter, I'm sure you related to them at some point. I'm sure something that you've went through in your life popped in your head. A time where you faced a struggle, but somehow found the power within yourself to just push through it.

As a coach, it's our job to preach that kind of thing to our teams during practices, pre-game talks, games, and post-game talks. We should have a desire in our hearts to take the lessons we have learned from failure, what it put us through, and how we got through it and tell it to your players. It doesn't matter when you tell them or how you tell them. Just tell them. And hope that they take just a small percentage of it away and keep with them. If they have done that, then you have done your job.

As a coach, you're the leader. And leaders should always lead by example because the people you are leading look up to you.

Speaking from the Heart

Just talk to them. Talk to them from your heart. Don't tell them anybody else's story but your own. It's your story, that very event on that very day that you remember like yesterday, that's going to connect to them the most. The one where failure was face to face with you, but you found a way to defeat it. The story when you truly learned the most about yourself. That's the story you need to tell because that'll make a difference and that's the definition of true power.

If you're looking for the right thing to say to get your team to overcome failure, this is your answer.

Failure is necessary, always remember that. And it's our duty to embrace it.

Digging Deep into the Roots of Failure

So, I know I keep saying how we need to embrace failure time and time again. And we do. But I feel like it can get a little confusing if you try to over think things. Which is what we all fall guilty to at one point or another.

Embracing failure is sometimes mistaken for desiring failure. I know they sound like the same thing, but they're not. They are completely different.

Let me simplify it for you and look at it like this. In our lives, we have wants and we have needs. The definition of a "want" is to feel a need or a desire for. It's something we would like to have, but there being no real benefit to us even if we did have it. A "want" and a "desire" are the exact same thing.

It's something that isn't necessary to us. Needing something is the exact opposite. The definition of a "need" is something deemed necessary. It's something we absolutely must have and will help us keep moving forward if we have it. That's exactly what I mean by "needing" to embrace failure.

Just remember, nobody has ever reached success in anything before first stumbling into failure.

CHAPTER 8

SMART RISK TAKING

We Take a Chance Every Day of Our Lives

Every morning when we wake up from a night's rest, get up, get ready, and drive to work, we take a chance. We take a chance that we'll make it to work safely without getting rear ended at a stop sign or t-boned at a four way intersection. We take that chance though because we have to, right? We don't really have a choice in going, because we know we have to make money to live. We have goals each year to make a certain amount of money so that one day, you'll have all of your bills paid off. We also have rewards that help us reach these goals as the weeks and months pass.

To reach a goal, we have to take risks and trust in the fact that we will be rewarded if we do things right. And given that it's our source of income, the decision for most of us is pretty simple. Go to work. Come home. Eat dinner. Relax. Go to bed. Wake up and do it all over again. Just like that, every day.

And I'm sure you're wondering right now what the heck my point is by telling you this, right? Because this is so simple and you feel like you're learning 1st grade math all over again. Not trying to hate on 1st grade though, because my granddaughter is in 1st grade!

My point is that this same thing applies to any kind of sports team or business. It comes down to four points that I just briefly discussed. And chances are, you might not even have picked up on it so that's why I'm going to break them down for you right now, one by one.

1. Knowing your plan
2. Knowing your risk
3. Knowing your reward
4. Making your decision

Before we played any game, we decided, as a group of coaches, on a plan to stick with for that game. We had to figure out the approach we were going to take to beat the other team. Through this, we figured out what players we were going to play, when to play them, and where to play them. Having a firm plan was important because it helped us measure our risks and rewards as the game went on. In turn, this allowed us to make better decisions for the team as a whole that would put us in a healthier position for winning the game.

In any game, situations are going to become present where taking a risk becomes necessary. In these types of situations, you have to first understand what the risk itself is, and how that it is going to affect you.

Let's Break It Down Further

Here, I'll use an example to help you better understand the importance of knowing your risk.

In baseball, it's a known fact that stealing third base as a baserunner is a challenge, to at least some extent, when facing just about any team. Well, unless you're playing the Bad News Bears! But no seriously, it is a high risk situation. In a situation like this, you have to understand what amount of loss you are putting at risk before you make any calls as a coach.

You also have to ask yourself if the risk you are considering is going to ultimately help you reach your goals. If it is, then it's a risk worth taking. If it's not, then it's not worth it. It's as simple as that.

So far I've talked about the first two things on the list. I've discussed having a plan and how to use that to your advantage. And I've talked about knowing your risk and knowing what your potential loss is.

The next step is knowing your reward. In other words, knowing how this risk is going to help you reach your goal.

Let's go back to the baseball example. Now, if you're not knowledgeable of all the ins and outs of baseball, that's okay. I am going to make sure it makes sense to you.

In the sport of baseball there are four bases. The majority of people know that, but if you didn't then that's okay because now you do. Between each base there is 90 feet. So total there is 360 feet.

Now, if I'm losing by one run near the end of the game, it's common knowledge that I need a run to tie the game and two to win. If I have a runner on 2nd base, he is 180 feet away from scoring. But on the other hand, if he steals to third base then that number is cut in half to 90, which puts him closer to scoring.

Common sense would tell anyone that I should at least think about taking the risk of him stealing third.

Now, if you are a baseball junkie then you probably understand that kind of situation depends on a number of different variables within the game. But, that's not the point of using that example. If you are anything like me you learn more from real life situations, not definitions and dried out concepts like some people like to teach.

The final part of becoming a smart risk taker is knowing your decision. This should, ultimately, be the easiest part because you have analyzed and thought through the risk at hand. You also realize the potential loss, potential reward, and how it effects and contributes towards your goal.

Again, as I have been reiterating over and over and over, these are things you can carry on with you throughout your entire life that will educate you and benefit you with making smarter decisions.

CHAPTER 9

HOW PRACTICE & PREPARATION IS A REFLECTION ON PERFORMANCE

Looking Back in the Rearview

After looking back on the 10 years of my life that I spent coaching the Angels, I'd love to know just how much time we spent as a team practicing and preparing for all those tournaments. All I can remember is practice after practice after practice, amongst countless hours working on their skills, techniques, and going over game situations so we would be ready for anything when it came game time.

Practice and preparation are important at all stages of life because the amount of practice and preparation that you put into something determines how well you perform.

As a coach, I've always believed in a tremendous amount of practice and preparation. Great habits and work ethic have always been a result that I've seen come out of it, so I stuck to doing it.

And I always had 4 distinct advantages that I tended to focus on, which led to the majority of success we had.

I always remembered these on my fingers, so I called it the Four Finger Rule. I'm going to break it down and simplify it for you, but first I'm going to list them together as a whole so you can see them visually.

> 1. Helps Polish Skills
> 2. Improves Team Chemistry
> 3. Useful for scrimmages or game situation simulations
> 4. Builds work ethic

Since I'm on the subject, I can't turn down the opportunity to include the most famous phrase of all time... Are you ready for this??

"Practice makes perfect."

You and I both knew it was coming. We've been taught this since we learned what yes and no meant as children. We've been taught by our parents, teachers, professors, coaches, mentors, etc. as our lives have progressed.

And there's a reason why we've heard it so much, because it's an easy three word sentence that sticks in our head like darn super glue and doesn't come out.

LEADING THROUGH LIVING

I wish I could deny this because it's just so plain-jane and typical to use, but I can't even begin to tell you how much I preached to the boys "Practice makes Perfect." I used it over and over and over. There was no need to get fancy. People like simple and simple works. So that's exactly how I kept it.

Let's Go Around the Horn

During practices, we had this drill called "Around the Horn." The players would split up into four even groups and each group would go to a given bag. I'd give them a baseball to throw around the bases to each other using proper mechanics and effort. I would make them throw it around the bases fifty times.

One time being around all four bases. If someone dropped the ball or threw it off line, we would start completely over and do it until we got it right. Sometimes this would get on the first time, but other times it might take us several attempts to get it right.

When you start to incorporate these types of challenges to a team, it more or less forces them to work together to achieve perfection. They begin to push each other to be better, even challenging each other, and it helps build the chemistry within the team. From this, players start to grow relationships with each other and the game starts to become more enjoyable because they appreciate their teammates.

One if the most effective strategies that always worked for us was committing a substantial amount of time to live scrimmaging. Sometimes we would just split the team up and do an inter-squad scrimmage. This proved to be effective in building competition between players competing for a certain spot or position. Scrimmages are times you want to set aside for evaluating your players and how well they react to live-game action.

Here and there, we would also go out and scrimmage another local team. While doing inter-squad scrimmages sort of helps more towards evaluating each of your players and their talents, scrimmaging other teams from time to time helps you identify how your team gels together, what fits where, and when it fits. Picture it like a puzzle. You have to put it together piece by piece, and certain pieces are just meant to fit at a certain place and time. You can't force it.

No matter where you are in life, there will always be things you need to apply these concepts to. Practice and preparation will always be a benefit to you. It's better to over-prepare than it is to under-prepare.

CHAPTER 10

Getting Where You Want To Be

I think one of the most important parts of living is having a plan. Having a plan that you're going to get up, go to work, and making sure you take care of certain things on your lunch break is a plan in itself, but that's sort of like a daily routine that you develop. I'm talking about something completely different. We all set goals in our lives, but yet we forget the most important part...

We don't have a plan that actually helps us achieve that goal, which is where it all starts. And I don't mean just a general idea in your head about something you want to pursue or work towards. I mean something real. Something written down on paper with daily, weekly, and monthly marks that you think are attainable for yourself.

And trust me, I know sitting down and actually doing this isn't easy. It's time consuming, you don't know where to start, and you feel like it wouldn't even actually help you achieve your goals even if you did sit down and do this. The "Quite frankly, it's just a waste of time" attitude that you'd rather spend your time scrolling through your Facebook News feeds filled with links to pointless articles and advertisements.

But I'm here to tell you, right here and right now, that constructing a plan will be the best thing you've ever done. I mean just ask yourself "Is it possible to work toward a goal without a plan?"

And surprisingly, the answer is yes. Sure it's possible. But what is actually going to keep you accountable when your focus starts to drift away from your goals? Is it an idea that's in your head? Or is it an idea that you have organized into a plan on a piece of paper that you see every day of your life?

It's got to be that plan on paper, 99.9% of the time. Having a plan on paper is the first step in the right direction when you're talking about reaching a goal.

It doesn't matter what your ultimate goal is, a plan is always necessary. Nobody reaches any kind of goal without taking steps to get there. It's just like a stair case, you can't just jump to the top. Well, I guess if you use the elevator you can! All kidding aside though, you get the point. It's step by step to the top. Step by step to where you want to be. Step by step to reach your goal.

Bringing a Plan to Life

During his internship, Hunter had to write out an extensive 12 page business plan months before even launching his business. He had to lay out a plan for which steps he would take in recruiting employees, marketing to the right community, traveling back and forth on the weekends, etc. He had set out for a long term goal of $50,000 in sales for himself, but he knew he would need a very focused and time lined plan to make that goal a living reality. With a full time college semester already on his plate, he knew his time management and organizational skills would need to be superior.

As to having a plan, Hunter says "putting a plan down on paper gave me an approach that dug down deep to the roots of my business. It allowed me to dissect each and every strategy to its core so that I could effectively succeed with my business when the time came. For me, it was kind of like building a railroad track. I thought of it as the time where I was piecing the track together so that when it was completely finished, it would keep my train on track to achieving my goals. That's kind of how I looked at it. I knew if I didn't lay my foundation down, I'd have no idea what I was doing."

Reap in the Benefits

Not only does having a plan benefit you by helping reach your goals, it becomes an advantage in three different aspects of your life:

Organization, Motivation, and Time Management.

As a result of having a plan, you will become more organized. You'll learn that it makes things easier on yourself when you have a plan. You don't want to be so stressed out about the little things.

By being able to visually see your plan, it helps motivate. It's a lot more powerful than just having that idea in your head I was talking about earlier. It is more powerful because it's right there for you to see. It's basically telling you to do it. And there's that little voice that's always in the back of your head saying that you spent the time to make the plan so follow through with it.

It's a motivator. And because you're motivated about this, you'll become more easily motivated with other things in your life.

The last thing that having a plan helps with is time management. You're going to see your time management skills improve tremendously. And it's not even because you're focusing on trying to improve in that area.

Organization, motivation, and time management all work together and as one improves, so does the other.

As you can see, having a plan for whatever goals you may have plays a tremendous role in achieving them, as well as other aspects of your life. If you don't have a plan, you might as well not even have a goal.

CHAPTER 11

SHORT MEMORY

Don't Let it Get You Down, Power Through

What exactly is it about making mistakes that gets us so down on ourselves? I mean, have we not yet come to the point of reality where we understand that nobody is perfect? Is that what it is? Or is it, that maybe we sometimes just try so hard for perfection that we let our mistakes get the best of us??

I don't know about you, but this happens to me all the time. I'm not here to tell you how perfect I am, because I'm not. What I'm here to tell you is how to fix that in yourself and in the people you are coaching. Because, I'm sure that you fall guilty to letting mistakes get the best of you, from time to time, just like I do.

Failing is frustrating, I know. Trust me. I've been there. And I've done that. I've been in your shoes. But now is not the time to quit, because I have the answer that is about to solve all of your problems.

To overcome any instance of failure, you must have short memory. This term is highly used by athletes amongst the sports world so if you don't know it means, that's okay. Short memory is simply just putting whatever just happened completely behind you and completely forgetting about it.

And to be honest with you, it doesn't matter if what just happened was a positive or a negative. You NEED to put it behind you. And I'm going to tell you exactly how to do that, in just a second. But before, I want to talk to you about something.

As much as we need to be focusing on fixing our mistakes every day, we tend to get a little caught up in it. This causes us to forget about just how much positive things can affect us. If we don't keep our self-control when success comes along, it could potentially hurt us worse than failure does. Just as have to put failure behind you, the same exact thing for success. Or else, you'll be putting a lot of things at risk. Things like your work ethic, humility, confidence, and so on. You DO NOT want to risk this. I'm sorry about that rant, I felt like it was necessary though.

LEADING THROUGH LIVING

Roller Coaster Riding Through it All

Having a short memory is great for roller coaster rides. And no, I don't mean the real theme park rides... Because roller coaster rides happen so fast you don't have a choice in the matter but to have short memory!

All kidding aside, I'm talking about the ups and downs we have every day of our lives. Real life situations. Whatever that may be for you. Whether it be at your job, coaching a little league baseball team, playing a sport as an athlete, or whatever. You understand. Being able to take what just happened and put it behind you is the most important thing. I can't reiterate this enough. Having that short memory is going to be to your benefit if you can follow these four simple guidelines.

1. Accept that you are going to make mistakes
2. Don't give into the negative voices
3. Learn from your mistakes
4. Use a routine to pick yourself up

Acceptance of Imperfection

First things first. We have to learn to accept that we are going to make mistakes. I'm not perfect. You aren't perfect. And neither is anyone else in this world. Except for my one year old granddaughter! She is something else now, let me tell you! Spoiled rotten!

But, we aren't perfect and we never will be. And if you're the kind of person who thinks you have it all figured out,

I'm here to break it to you. It's all going to come tumbling down on you, at some point. You better be careful and go humble yourself before it gets you.

The moment that we accept imperfection is the very moment that doors begin to open up for us. It's the idea of having a forward mindset instead of a backwards mindset. The idea of being in the "Here and Now" moment and always looking forward for what's ahead. No train has ever reached its destination by going backwards, remember that one.

And remember this too. Nobody expects you to be perfect. Just be the best version of yourself that you can possibly be.

Blocking out the Voices

The second thing is, don't give into the negative voices. And there are two kinds of voices. There are going to be the voices inside of your head giving you self- doubt and telling you that you can't achieve your goal. And there are outside voices. These voices are of people who surround you, maybe your peers or competitors. And some of them are going to try to bring you down. Don't listen to them though, take them as a grain of salt. Or like fairy dust, which doesn't even exist. But don't tell your child that! You listening to them is just you stooping down to their level. You don't want to do that. Why? Because you're better than that.

With the inner voices trying to give you the devil talk, you have to keep that forward mindset I was talking about a few minutes ago. If you can be consistent with staying positive, then those negative voices are going to fade farther and farther away.

Not Making the Same Mistake Twice

The third thing is, learn from your mistakes. How many times have ever made the same mistake twice and then slapped yourself for it? Probably a lot right? Hey, it happens. We're humans, after all. Not robots.

You are going to make mistakes, but you need to learn from each and every one of them so that you won't make the same mistake twice. Assess what you did wrong and figure out what you need to correct so that it doesn't happen again.

The Traditional Pick-Me-Up Pep Talk

The fourth thing is, have some kind of routine for picking yourself up when making a mistake. It doesn't have to be anything fancy, just something simple that works for you. For example, a lot of football players like to slap their helmets to kind of give themselves a wake-up call. Or for me, I like to give myself a little inner pep talk for a few seconds so I can reverse my mindset. Everyone develops their own little thing that helps them. You just have to find what it is. You might already know. And if you do, that's great! It makes your life a heck of a lot easier, as you've probably already come to find out!

All four of these things are very important in the process of having a short memory. They all work together as one and one can't operate without the other.

If you follow each of the four guidelines that I have talked about in this chapter, you will find yourself edging closer and closer to the goals you are trying to reach.

CHAPTER 12

#DOITFOR3

Heroes Will Be Remembered, But Legends Never Die

Each of the lessons I have discussed in the previous eleven chapters depend on each other to make winning a reality at the end of the day. If you are lacking in one area, it is going to have an effect on you in other areas.

If you can remember back to the first chapter, I told you about Trevor, the young man who we dedicated this book to. Trevor was a special kid. He was the kind of person who could light up the dark. And his smile was infectious to anyone who was around him.

Trevor was always #3 while he played for us and that's why I have given this chapter the title #DoItFor3. And we also purposefully designed the outline of this book to have a total of 12 chapters. Our drive behind that is 1 + 2 = 3, obviously 3 being Trevor's number.

Trevor adopted the nickname "Rooster" while he played with us. And it's a pretty hilarious story how that came about.

He had this little dance he would do from time to time where he would move his legs really fast! It always reminded me of how Elvis used to dance on stage.

As he did his little dance one day during practice, some of the players found it quite amusing. That was just like Trevor! One of the players said it looked like a rooster, by the way his legs were moving, one day and that's how the name "rooster" came about!

He played with us for many years, so as you can imagine, we grew very close to him and his family. His father, Allen, was one of my assistant coaches for several years. We shared more memories than we can even remember.

Tragedy Out of Nowhere

About two years ago though, something awful happened. Early hours in the morning of June 15th, 2013, Trevor had a tragic incident and unfortunately passed away. I'd rather not talk about what exactly happened because it's so personal to his family and also us.

LEADING THROUGH LIVING

To be honest, I'll never forget that day.

It was easily one of the worst days of my entire life. I'll never forget being woken up at 7am by my wife yelling across the house that Trevor had passed away. It was that very moment that changed my life forever.

I would have never guessed as I lied down the night before, that something so tragic would happen just a few hours into the morning.

It just didn't seem real. It felt like a nightmare and that I was just waiting on someone to wake me up from it.

It absolutely crushed us. Trevor had been over at our house just a few weeks before, playing guitar with Hunter. And just months before that, Allen, Trevor, Hunter, and I went to the strip club for some fun! It was Hunter's first time going so it was an awesome experience!

These were just a couple memories that we shared together prior to his death, aside from the years of baseball spent together. But, suddenly everything had changed.

Him passing away made everything different. My perspective on life changed forever. It's made me realize just how fragile life can be. These days, it seems like you just can't take anything for granted.

Getting Caught In the Chaos

All of those years spent coaching the Angels appear so differently to me now. Looking back, there were too many times where, as a coach, I was so focused on winning, I would get frustrated or upset when the team didn't perform like I had wanted.

But now, I feel like a fool for that. Because now, I realize the truth of it all. It was all just a game. We were just out there making memories that would last us a lifetime and we didn't even know it. We would often get so caught up in the chaos of winning and playing perfect baseball, it would take a toll on all of us.

Proper Perspective

No matter where you are in life, please don't lose sight of your family and friends. That is what is most important at the end of the day. Although I did preach this a lot to my players, there were certainly moments that got the best of us. We weren't perfect. But, that's just the nature of life.

Things aren't going to always go your way. You just have to accept that.

It is important to keep a proper perspective on things that happen in life because it's going to help you in the long run.

My message to you is don't sweat the small stuff. Know that every day you wake up from a good nights rest is a day that some people don't get the opportunity to have. I don't think it is possible to truly understand just how fragile life is until something tragic happens in your life, like it did to us.

So, I have one last thing to say.

And that is to tell your family you love them. Tell them you care about them. Tell your team you love them. Tell them you care about them too.

Tell your friends you love them. And tell them you care about them. You just never know when the last time you'll see that person is going to be. That's the full and honest truth.

Because at the end of the day, its love that makes this world go around. And you truly never know when the last time you'll see somebody will be.

Angel in the Sky

I committed this chapter to Trevor, telling his story, and the impact he had and still has on my life. Over the past two years, I have felt uneasy about his death. I didn't feel like there was any closure.

But now, I feel like this has been the exact answer I've been looking for. Writing this book as a tribute to him is exactly what I needed.

When we first founded the Myrtle Beach Angels, I wasn't sure why I had wanted "Angels" to be the name of our team. But, it makes sense now. That's for sure. Trevor was an Angel with us then, but he is an Angel FOR us now!

What Will You Take Away?

Out of the 11 life lessons that I have preached on throughout this book, I hope you have been able to take something away from it. Even if it was only one sentence in this book, I feel like my job is done. It wasn't easy putting all of my experiences into just 12 short chapters, but I truly hope it helps you, your team, or business succeed in wherever this crazy thing called life takes you.

Just so you can see them one last time, I'm going to list them out for you:

1. Humility
2. Discipline
3. Intimidation
4. Confidence
5. Hard Work Beats Talent, When Talent Doesn't Work Hard
6. Embracing Failure
7. Smart Risk Taking
8. Practice & Preparation
9. Having a Plan
10. Short Memory
11. It's Just a Game

LEADING THROUGH LIVING

So as we begin to part ways here, think about those 11 life lessons and what you can do to apply them to your life. I can promise you that you'll see success come your way if you follow the guidelines that I have laid out for you throughout these 12 chapters. I truly hope you've enjoyed this book! Hunter and I wish you well wherever you go in life!

You can reach us at huntergoff@leadinthroughlivin.com if you need us!

HOLD UP, HOLD UP

Get a laugh out of these nicknames we had!

Top (Left to Right): Iggy Cossentino (Igg-ster), Joshua Long (JL), Roger Goff (Roger-Dodger), Nick Franza (Godzilla), Trey Keller (Bambi), Aaron Beebe (Beebs), Jim Davis (Jimbo), Michael Hodge (Big Mike), Hugh Benton (HughB), Jared Rickman (J-Rod)

Bottom: Tanner English (Sweet-T), Ryder Tipton (Ryder-Cup, Ice Cream), Anthony Cossentino (AC, Ant), Hunter Goff (Hairy-George), **Trevor Worden (Rooster)**, Allen Worden (Coach Allen)

ROGER & HUNTER GOFF

Top (Left to Right): Roger Goff, Richard Carmichael (Flash), Jacob Simmons (Jake-the-Snake, Crazy-Jake), Hugh Benton, Trey Keller, Hunter Goff, Iggy Cossentino

Middle: Joshua Long, Josh Powell (Rex), Nick Franza, Francis Chock (Chock)

Bottom: Cary Messer (Boo), Anthony Cossentino

Not Seen: Travis Shelley

Thank you for reading our book!

We really appreciate all of your feedback, and we love hearing what you have to say.

We need your feedback to make the next version better. Please leave us a helpful REVIEW on Amazon letting us know what you thought of the book.

Thanks so much!

Roger & Hunter Goff

We love you Trev #DoItFor3